Other Side of Sea
海之彼岸

Other Side of Sea
Xiaoqiu Qiu

Etchings Press
Indianapolis, Indiana

This publication is made possible by funding provided by the Shaheen College of Arts and Sciences and the Department of English at the University of Indianapolis. Special thanks to the students who judged, edited, designed, and published this chapbook: Mackenzie Hyatt and Sam Jackson.

UNIVERSITY *of*
INDIANAPOLIS.

Published by Etchings Press
1400 E. Hanna Ave.
Indianapolis, Indiana 46227
All rights reserved

etchings.uindy.edu
www.uindy.edu/cas/english

Printed by IngramSpark

Published in the United States of America

ISBN 978-1-955521-31-4
27 26 25 24 23   1 2 3 4 5

Cover image by Thomas Nordwest
Cover design by Mackenzie Hyatt
Interior design by Mackenzie Hyatt and Sam Jackson

Cover text is set in Onyx, Pristina, and Lora.
Interior texts are set in Lora and Ma Shan Zheng.

Contents

out of Target's automatic doors
the sky is heartbreaking blue green boat thing
that a crushed coke can
tap dance
between the parking lot arrows pointing different angles
knows, this
is the edge of the world
waves of moon splashes
down its teeny tin ridges
drunk red decks
into each other
every light
of the night
tilts, I
can barely hold on
to this question,
cold wind in a desert
is from the sea:
two petals of calypso orchid
kiss tremblingly
at its lee

---

[1] "*Hwra*", Old Chinese for "flower"

My Morning that is Lunar New Year's Eve

then I think, I should
be there, holding the love
and scorn of my relatives'

gaze about why I still haven't got
married, rather that than the stare
from this anthology, these alien letters

squirming like mosquito larvae
in the yellowed pages like toilet bowl
water, I am ashamed to care
for their meaningful twitch

about love and truth, I miss small,
muddy words, perhaps half stuffed with
fish-meat ball, asking indistinct, but in fact,
mad at someone for not clearing the cabbage
bowl for the chickens, the infant-like

wordplay, the simple intricacy of emotion and
intellect, makes me never have to

think—but wish
to answer it, even from the other side
of a poem, and go

down to the hens, and fumble in the dark for the
switch, and feel sad for myself, turning 30 and all,
and my younger brother, hand me over his newly born, flick

the light, and smile, on, thaws my guilt, unbearable
but warm, the sunlit dew on tender morning leaves

the baby, soundly, how we used to think we don't
know how to hold one. It is these dampened frames
we stand under, not us, that outlive time, (tonight,
mine a window paper white that cuts me, yours
painted red for newly-wed), that

we look out, eyes un-aged, gives the wideness
back to the world, cold sea frees our gaze
and shoulders fall on the edges
in light thuds

between the two,
we become the moon

Untitled #87

deep beneath
the canopy

a bright shadow
plunge

on a tiny leaf,
fresh, tender

a green
on the whole brown branch

every grown leaf
churns in the wind:

it tilts slowly
with their beat

Leaving the English Department

tonight, many roads in this city should
be jammed,
I hear the soft cold winds as I descend
the stairs

they have put small roses at the crevices
of the beams,
one to another in unequal distances,
looking

somewhere the street lights come up splays
heavily the windows,
people go on breathing into
the heat with their faces

we pass each other,
you make yourself not look
at me,

my heartbreaks both ways.
I shut the door

very much behind me, and ahead
the small pine cone stands in the middle

of the road, its cruel contours
against the thin moon

PHOTONS

If the faster I travel the slower time ticks for me, and we dreamed of one another at the opposite side of the earth. When. The bookspines I carried all the way from China peeling off freshly. This morning somebody has to ask, what is your age? This particular moment will be felt old approximately two years later. Our timelines are recommended and therefore are never ours. Secretly, someone finally confesses to me at the water fountain they dream about towering mosques and fire breeding calderas they have never been to. I realize I do not miss home, I miss neverlands. I dreamt and believed the bookstore I frequented as a child will survive whatever erratic weather the planet has in store for us. I feel safe when the texts stay there no matter how much I run my fingers. To dream about a place is to wake up to a crack in time. In one of the chunky hard-covered science books I learned about photons. They travel 40,000 years to touch the blackness of our eyes at the speed of light. They themselves never age. Time stops for them. I finally went back home to China after five years and the bookstore was gone. It had been gone for ten years.

Woman on a High Stool, Matisse, Las Vegas

only where the shadow is
on a vaulted bank, water is black
and thin, before streams down
to the spare spaces of trash
the riverbed, it shines blue, skirted
sky against strokes of teal, half-pleated
bushes, edges hollow out, the wooden
cityscape: I don't know who she is—
but I have known them. That look. They wrap
their entire, chromatic life behind
a sweat-saturated black, and wait with
clasped hands, tinted by
some sclera-eating sun
on the strip, a tourist guy confesses
he's scared of homeless artists
singing aggressively, to TV news
cut to exterior, day, wide shot of
a group of them
unsure if should get up
from their always gray carpets, gray
that rams through their scarves, ropes,
paint-peeled banisters and the front ceramic
tiles of Caesars Palace, and if the grey has toned
them, or they it, and
to the audience behind the frame, if
there's something they're supposed to say.

Untitled #24

Moon   stops   wind-leaves

the palm   shadows   move   a long   crack on

the parking lot   drunkard   on   sunroof

      I am in the way.

The 3rd Graders Go to School

How far am I from the truth?
All I have are two LED screens of opposite news
glaring like unsheathed blades,
and some broken words of a phone call
from a friend who still lives in Hong Kong.
I am two worlds away, and the
birds here sing so differently in the morn.
I can never get used to
a turquoise colored dawn.
But every time I want to hold on
to something like a truth,
I think of them. I remember
how they marched down the narrow roads,
chilly and quiet in the early morning,
how they have to pass
four times the customs,
two in Shenzhen and two in Hong Kong,
and walk two hours straight,
just so they can make it
to the morning recitals,
their school classrooms at Kowloon.
I imagine them marching down
the burnt street,
in their snow-white uniforms
and flapping Red Scarves.
One of them got peanut butter on his dimple
the shape of a tiny star.
I imagine
tiny shoes wobbling in concert,
like dandelions barely holding on
at the softest touch of a wind;
and the colorful lunchboxes!
Teal green, navy blue,
blue, blue with stripes, yellow and red,
packed by their moms at 4 a.m.
4 is before the birds and bikes, I imagine,
before the honks and engines,

roadblocks and sirens,
chants and shouts,
locked arms and bent knees;
before the "we"s and "them"s,
and the smoked air and the startled pigeons.
Before anything.
They march from their average homes in Shenzhen,
and I imagine it is not a crucial difference
for any of them, that words
don't mean something.
The flags roaring in the wind
have an ideal to teach.
The smeared plaques on the ground
did an age wrong.
The giant strokes of characters
clinks and clanks on...
I imagine they walk on
and their feet know only
the next firm, solid ground.
I see their little but sharp eyes
waiting at red lights,
reaching for the world.
One by one, and always before
not after, a decision, they take it all in:
the colors of angry laser pointers
and of a dewed roadside rose,
equal, to their unmasked noses.
I imagine a boy would pick a rose
as they wait at the traffic, and put it
in a girl's hands, well before
they learn its name at school;
before the redness
takes hold—it is already safely
in her palm—I imagine
they march on, perhaps singing
a song, knowing only half the lyrics,
a song that neither the chess-playing old man
nor the bulbar birds, nor the loudspeakers
will recognize, but can't help to hum along.

A song sung mostly out of tune, or even jarring
to some. And perhaps a hurrying figure
who rushed to the metro, I imagine,
who moved by their earnest and simple tune,
might stop, and give it a listen—
In my imagination, truth is not hard.
It does not ask you anything,
doesn't ask you to swear fealty, or be its gunman,
nor does it blockade you
or hold a grudge against other truths.
In my imagination, truth
is not far from the third graders,
infallibly every morning,
go to school.

[this sweet little word]

"Doch unsere Liebe
heißt sie nicht Tristan
und – Isolde?
Dies süße Wörtlein: und
was es bindet
der Liebe Bund"

This reed stalks in my hand, bends
still like the thousands of others
I did not pick
on the bank, the gray sands
the long river ends
the mist, bird shadows
the strands, the stones wait
and dies
in the white. I think
about the long voice messages
my mom sends me, the concerns
that ask no reply, the message bubbles one
and the next, the space in between, the long river, the
sea, and the drizzle starts, the each duck and
every rainstring, adjacent by another.

Cormorant at Chicxulub Crater

Along   the   sun

   and   clouds

the cormorant   drifts

up
   and   down

   up
    and   down

light

   and solid

   like a   seed,

the ocean   tilts

and spilled   over

a few   continents:

it flaps

and   drops down

   a poop

The Little Dying

I sit alone with twenty other people in a ketch-up colored restaurant
   with ketchup chairs and ketchup counters and ketchup on the
   table, attempt to feel
The moment I have no words to describe, this little town who dubbed
   itself as the biggest small town on Route 66, and the apocalyptic
   sunsets in western Arizona
White lights sprayed on the drops of Tabasco lid, the pale of the tuna
   eyes on the bathroom poster, and this guy next to my table whose
   grey hair chisels in his cap back "U.S.A"
My grandpa would call this *zen ya vu tang*, in his earthly Wu, "the wilds of
   fairies," or "the most bizarre," it took little to qualify as strange if you
   lived your whole life along a river
The sirloin gets a clean cut, fully dusted with colors, sprawled to all edges
   of the plate, and curls up two bloated mouth sacks. Everything here
   wouldn't settle for a tad less than maximum
When my father assured me as he sprinkled his plants from the side and
   dipped unevenly to leave room for the sun and decay, that grandpa was
   gonna overcome it, I was fully convinced
On my way here, layers and layers of Permian sediments flurried on both
   sides of freeway, rocks red like dying stars, from an age when volcanos
   erupted for millennia and all life almost died
I'm just worried about my nephew in Hangzhou. He looked like a kid king
   with amazing extra-curricular talents and when we spoke in
   Wu Chinese, he replied in impeccable Mandarin
Even my old classmates when we had our rare reunion in closed quarters
   in chic Shanghai dumpling shops that no other table could overhear,
   they swallowed their Wu like hot soup
My coworker Lily sent me this beautiful green Boston Celtics themed
   birthday card with ivies but I later learned she added all the "r"s when
   teaching, and at bars, and in life, in general
Tonight I have the whole desert to myself, its ashtray skin, flammable like
   dry parchments, all ten libraries of them, and all these extra utensils
   that are way too clean
All of them, like small, strangely shaped snowflakes, itchy, but coldless,
   on my face, and I have nowhere to begin to mourn, when I got the
   message an ocean away, my grandpa is no more

I had imagined death to be a Great Dying, tears of shooting stars
and sound of earthquake cries, while the sanded wind bashed its
skull on this pane, unceremonious, soundless, on my end
In thirty years Wu will go extinct, the city folks say, I always
wondered if I will watch it go, or am watching, or am going, step
by step, it
And I stand up and starts to walk backwards, step by step, and trace
every little dying along the way that proves me alive, out of the
door, until the blowing sand hit my cheeks like sunrise

Untitled #95

ぼう
"Bō"
could mean
:

帽
a Hat

望
Full Moon,
Observe

坊
a Boy,
a Monk

暮雨
Evening Rain

某
Someone
Somewhere; I, Me

棒
a Bar,
a Staff

房 a Room, a Monastery

暴 Violence, Illegality, Unreasonableness

貌 Appearance, Complexion; Shape and Form

Then,

The Monk Boy

Somewhere   above his hat,

Evening rains,   the complexions of

Him, full moons/   observes,

A violence/   an illegality,

his own broom   sweeps

The room/   the monastery,

The only other   sound.

first date

you didn't venmo me the pho
we had together, this spring
gets away being steamily cold
for whole three months, I blamed
the hard seedcoats that buxom its way
out of white almond flowers, you are rain
for sticking in the middle of my poems, where I want to say
I like you a lot lot, it keeps me sprouting
concealed metaphors, like a boy
practices saying "take my hand" to fallen ivies, or
to the red bricked wall, where green verges
at the fingerpresses of shadows
patter branches,
you and the afternoon sun how always progresses:
I have to keep guessing what I did wrong—
Should let images stay
objects, a second too long,
the last two sections of a paper opens
before the plastic bags swivel
into ballet, the tiny raindrop crouches
on the window, in case the small wind
tapping for it to punctuate,
and the quivering snowdrop petals
I skip, like moth
when I come everything to see you, running
into me tell me you want to
make
that lunch on the last day of spring
our first date

Old Havana Wall

above
empty cartons
and cans
black and bold
:

        ¡NO Arrojar Escombros!

        delegado p.p.
        P.N.R
        C.D.R

all about the broken
bricks, bags, bottles
scrawls
blacksprays:

        a/b
          2+2=5
            4!

                    re__ ion!
                ¡sí _e pue__ !

the dark, fresh, stuff
of

it
rains again
the flower drooling
pink
on the blackbin

a heart
pounding
and pounding

it rains heavier

100 Pages of Proust Due on Chinese New Year's Eve

right now
i cannot   bear to read
my proust
that little   patter of
firecracker
in my phone,   heels on
Cobble stone
at my heart
I've to walk,   all with you
monsieur proust
tonight, to your signs
I am thinking
fuzzy, bunny ears
and my nephew's finger
under   the rabbit pen
their small entirety
threads in between
winter   sunbeam, unaware
of my imagination
and nearly spilled   pumpkin soup
grandma brings   from the farm
snow sleeps   under a string
of footprints, crisp and murmuring
certainty, and each and single
of their good news! Spring
festival lanterns,   free   red tassels
dangle   at the edges
of last few oranges   a sun
setting,   so full
of ourselves   and the old years
still warm,
he takes   a sip, and cries
hot   hot
grandma smiles
for a while, I have lost
you, M. Proust,
in your Petit Phrase

in your smoke-fumed room
I am thinking
Home
the other end of ocean
and what would happen
if you   and I,
don't have to make them little words
 stand
for something, and lower
their first sound,
would the milky way be less
accidental
I open up the window
and let them all   go
at once, one
and one, and I
send them crackle
and explode
in a smoke:
com   bray
bal bec
gil bert
robert
verdu
-rin,
guer-
mantes
perdu
prin-
temps
temps
temps
temps...

Sunflowers in Soup

"Kveld lifir maðr ekki
Eptir kvið norna."
("A man does not live a single evening
After the decree of the fates.") – Poetic Edda

In that moment, you're
naked: it did not
present, but disguise
Strokes
after color-
ful strokes, it is always
half and more
than what it stems:
the dying cannot commiserate
the guilt of the dead;
they have their own decay, petal
after petal, to hide behind.
only in the rich, spontaneous cata-
strophe, death becomes meta-
phoric, the tawny seed beds discharge
A dark remorse
of the kneeling figure: the vividness
of it, the dying laid level
with the dead, the discoloring backdrops—
this has always been the painting
Every day, when death comes
with its pre-sketched yellow edges, you
the leaf that grows beside
it, no less bright and full enough
to fall.

Untitled #45

Evening symphony
at the Coliseum
the conductor
and his hands.
The flock of birds above
dashes
and turns, in one
without lead
and without end.

Birthday Alone

I poured three eggs onto the plate
another birthday coincided with Thanksgiving day
except this is my thirtieth, and per my mom
my birthday on the lunar calendar also coincided today
so three eggs for three coincidences, per tradition,
I opened my kitchen door
and the two little gnats or flies, or wachumacallit
rushing pass me like children seeing presents,
they probably waited outside for the whole fifteen minutes,
while I attempted to break the shells—
they were tougher than air, some egg flakes,
like the darker fields of Rothko
fell into the yoke, and became quite elusive
every time I tried to scoop them up they
scattered and spurted in their fishy ways
some must've escaped
and sat through the sizzling of my pan
matter-of-factly, like this whole time my eyes
spellbound
on how a pair of my close friends from fifth grade got married
and cheated on each other just as violently how
my younger cousin's boy did cry
the exact the same way as she used to how
an innocent and inseparable friend of mine, how I cursed
and missed his innocence, stopped talking to me after
his father's suicide, and I alone at the other end
of the ocean, fifteen minutes later, watching the flies
dance and buzz, two small, solid speckles
between the churning and twisting lines
of steam, then land
soundlessly beside me, stilling the two pieces of world
divided by its wings: how
my entire lived life is smaller than this moment

the flower duet

that we can't breathe in it
      makes it   the sea
and so are the pair of car lights
        opens
          and closes
and closes
       and opens
through the lamp poles
             bioluminescent
we're barred from their conversations
     a cloud cumulus is only *told*
       apart from a cirrus
they are more   pothos whose
untrimmed fingers sign two words
a day
   close and
open,   like
          jellyfish
all the lights on the hills palpitates   around
I   am too small to see them move.
What makes the starless sky a
 dead sea, makes us
reflections:
the magic is   not   there there
(the night is too contiguous to be there)
when I closes,   they opens
(I alone dark petals, everywhere opens)

Purpose of Visit

Because a past me is not departed enough for me to write about, I fold inward across the sea zigzag a brown bamboo leaf to placehold as an object of grief. This provides temporary proof to an ancient dichotomy of light of my eyes and the light that casts my shadows. I came here alone. Only a California thrasher got trapped inside the airport, we feel its always frantic colors. Every piece of dome promises a sky but none gives the blue exit. The ex-statically expressive track of its small, charged fluttering. Needles. As a kid, my mom encourages me to use my hand to aid my speech as if words are better felt on fingertips. I hold every morning mist through window mesh as white fingers of well-said, undocumented secrets of a love immemorial. Any documentation required in life presupposes small cuts on your skin, as you fit your uneven, love-beaten torso through its geometric edges. All knives are cast by another knife and therefore is never whole. I almost re-member them. When my dad brought a blue holed plastic bag of milk cartons to see me in boarding school, I had made a difference between interior sadness, which was the blood-soaked, rectangular slowcut of dusk-light across the dry snailshells, their hollow secrets spleening all across the dull white wall, and an exterior one. The skills to fold, however, gives such an im-penetrable disguise that the inside of the paper is never a question of the origami once you have decided which point to fold against. I at this not tell my dad the night before I had a knife on my neck. It was about the same temperature as a pen. At the same time, if you come over to the other side of the skin, you will see the writing grow. When asked to sign, I realize I have never written right in front of anyone except me. Unlike truth, secrets are told pretty much the same shape to someone else. Still only one side of them tingles. When they do, they do so like mountains. Other students pretend to pass by, as I cried sheets and sheets of rice papers on the second calligraphy class. It halos the ink and therefore foot-

"mi": secret; calmness atop mountain...

"mi": calmness; a rooftop (home) over this certainty

"bi": certainty; a laceration over the heart

"xin": heart

prints on soft snows. All rituals are private in nature. It is okay. The depth is from heart to hand, not the front and back of paper. Take your time. The only certain thing you know is the wound. A kind of firm clinch, the grip between tiles on roof-slants, on my arm every time me and my dad at traffic lights. We let our past run ahead but they always turn back to hold our hands. Lead on. We rode on the seat and back of a bike to move to the city. I and all the grasshoppers I take with me in the bottle knows I love. By moving them away I killed them. I begin to see the rationales of mass extinctions. I have no contacts in the next world. If only regrowth depends on perishability. The coil of rain. The angle of clouds. The rustle of dirt. My wounds have grown like a wall. I have raised them like a child. These are my dependents. My timid self crouching like a riverbed before you. My torment self giving way like a glacial moulin behind you. I thought I got good at killing. The knife grows glows growls inside me and I am wielding it willing it to undivide me. That, it cannot do. Running away equals running into. Here goes an ocean. Here goes a decade. Here I am. On the inside, the laceration of the wound is visible in the sky like a galaxy, a billion stars, glittering from horizon to horizon, imagine all the colors you have never seen before. All you need are a few fingertips and the names of walls and a dome. Fold your legs against the universe. Say, thanks for inviting. I am going home.

Untitled #48

earphone cord as-ifs on my sheet, there are
no words in english for "long rivers" as in Yangtze
mountains and mountains
my arms around my kneecaps

("wan": as if/winding)

Parasol Leaves on Urumqi Road

I don't know how they
synchronize, each
blade vibrates
toward a different angle, but
a stem stuck in the crevice once
the entire wind
is off balance—they didn't
fall, they rub their deep, complete
wings on the cement,
raise, and unraise,
stuck and unstuck,
then breaks, turns, opens wide,
and folds, kneels, and embraces tight
then lies down, eyes down, softly the
ground, necks bend, as if lips, coarsely
the ground, and one, and two
of them, only bare stems, small, quick
spins, twists, summersaults every
turn, they burn, and crackle, and woosh,
and swirl, and whizz, but break, but burn,
but grow, and grow—
until the rain, despite the rain, because the rain.

the more they lie flat
louder
they splatter
the rain

Catalina

"Mira que me voy a morir..."

some times along University Center Drive
and after she left me,
an old mesquite tree next to a smaller tree.
a dandelion, a loaf of chartreuse and all
the glittering gravels and sands surround it

a moment and
the cars and planes scurry through
Saturday morning, pieces of sun
smuggle away on their dark windows

beside all of them, a very blue tent
between the two trees, when I pass by
we slow us down

the clouds

leaves no wind, how every-
one dies by oneself,
the crows leering
the tattered-clothes sauntering back
the police car engine mad

Untitled #13

mountains   mountains
    of ink clouds
collapse upon
     the   horizon

   under the
     green   gazebo
a pigeon   peck peck
seeds

Indeed, the loud wham of the sudden moon

cat flea

from a dream i wake up
and find the worst news in china
from america, and the worst
in america, from china, one admits
freely: "your heaven has no god" and the other
acknowledges in candor: "your god lives not
in heaven"
one calls the other a hate praiser,
the other calls one
a vice ambassador, graciously
they'll help each other build
a new Eldorado, another Shangri-La
except the world is already ugly,
and the people are
always sad—
"at least they agree the weather
is getting too hot," and the coffee mugs
made in china are—to quote my cat,
nyah-whaah. And even she is
not having it, sprawl out like a pile of toffee
wrapping
at the edge of the dark sofa, white patches giving
up, like small, flying
puffs above sierra,
you'd think some snow caps heard
the call, and took off
to their grandpa like mothership, but shhh, listen!
holding onto one
of the corners of white
of the peak, a hare, candle-furred
with its entire and wistful snout, fully pressed, upon snow surface
tsk tsk   tsk tsk   tsk tsk
then raises, piously, joins its two palms, and nose
bobbing, tickling, the air
original as the move, and then
again, down it went, nibbling the softening snow
as if, in the inertia of half-awakenness, choreographing

a dream, a sincerity, self-starting
telescoping, all the snows that fell, and is fallen,
under
ground, murmurs a constellational
news: this is what we have, and
this is just enough
to the next spring
to the next calamity
this is the same dream that they shall have
and have gotten
wrong
yawns my cat, as she—
cutting my poem
short—
uncurls and crumbles
all the little dreamy peaks and mythlings
that lives itchily on her fur, and in fact
and facts
demand, a dousing bath,
as if to say:
"wash'em, wash'em away
they're not mine anymore than they're
yours,"
so i took her to the tub, and gave
her a shower, but even then, even
at that very moment of factuality
she didn't resist, nor did she
gnarl or snarl or try
to run away, like a cat, i imagine
would

Untitled #39

After a wettest winter

       April.

Desert of real.   (There is no here there.

    ten   thousand   young   tumble   -   weeds

wait

   like a map.
                A
                   small
              stream
                  of
              broo
                   k
                     nec
             k
                    ing
               be
             t
             ween

           gasping—
            —gagging

                        a green-tailed gecko
                        lick-lick its eyeball

snowline   perches   like a dead owl

              A triangle roadsign
              faded red edges
              missingacorner
               r e   a ds
               VVIND

The Cleaner on Zócalo

It's lunch time so she goes for a patrol under the bright shoulders
pass by clamorous street like dead leaves on a river flows listless
she put on her neon green suits the olive psychedelic graffiti snake-
head on the lime-plastered wall of a McDonald clay-red she first
walks to the lidless paper cup with a bite mark on the cusp hides a
fruit fly over there the couple that dumped it still shines
under the hot sun where she patiently clamps it and decants it and
flattens it and makes it disappear into her wastecart meltable in
the heat-bent air a Subway wrapper clings to a drainage grate like a
palm in some ancient process of sinking when picked up grease and
saliva climbing over her hands are obsidian tan reflecting sunrays
dashes from screen to screen at the intersection heads looks down
their phones with fingers swaddling it's 1:10 she swaddles away her
long braids around her neck sticking down gazing quietly into the
big black bin right at the center of the city if it is in the city and can
be thrown away she's seen it all the colors and hues congregate in
the bottom she rakes out a half-black egg carton and a plastic water
bag and a warm napkin-wrapped corn-stick out of it is a dead crow
she flips it and lays it on top of the sorted pile beak skyward for a
while and pushes her cart away from the hurrying high heels and
Nikes comes a drumbeat on the square her sisters gather in Nahua
attire for the harvest of this year arranging barleys and wheat ears
in the shape of Sun radiating in that direction she sweeps the spot-
less street with a broom and makes sure no one sees when close
enough she gives one of the rays
a little prune

Untitled #108

where between the barbs, iron
pupils, angular, thinking, the crow

land projects—concave, cordon
to diagonal, trackwayed, and hard

its uneven feathers taper to a point
the sierra ridges are black, bent

it shakes its head, the machine
neck, horizontal

Naturaleza Muerta

but I dare not / put her into the picture:
she looked me / so calmly,

with a dark curiosity, and a bright melancholy.
her chubby guacamaya eyes / have discovered

my secret, I think.
I could, however, put her back

easily, together with two hundred other kids
Mestizos or Nahuas / in jolly green suits,

and the forbiddingly purple / jacaranda trees.
Put them all under / that dark dense statue

around which they gather, how
they were told to look up / with their nascent eyes,

to this / last king of Spain,
last king of New Spain, first king of Mexico.

and I could zoom in / on his charcoal fingers,
as raw and as seasoned / as a skeleton,

clenching to a burnished scroll (*Mexica,*
your tribal name shall be restored)

whose giant shadow like a sword
swinging over / a plaza of bright, curious noses

and side by side, objects are aligned:
the dead fingers / and the conquest that lives on

the live gazes / and the "*perdón*" to a mother tongue
some natures dead / only on the outside,

others survive, only / on the outside.
perhaps even, a cold wind

might blow by, smoothening
any recalcitrant / leaves, and all the shades

will unify. but I dare not
put her into the picture.

I'm afraid that she might hear
my tacit, unpermitted

scribing of her, and all
my presumed measurements

of her, root, appearance, and hope
flaw, innocence, and toil,

will vaporize / and the gleeful
resignation / to a unison of colors

will be destroyed / like cicada's wing
under / a meteoroid

I'm afraid of the invitationness
of her eyes / that of no history

that of no language
that of no verdict

as the ice sheets on a cliff / collapsing
into the welcoming sea

when looking / at me
will invite me

to join her human look,
her looking at me, no less,

a man-shaped blank / inside
his own still life

and I closed my eyes—
             "¡Mira! ¡Un fotógrafo!"

into central Shanghai on the only bus

After, I didn't recognize
what they were
gesturing, but the roadside tree
branches
sway passionately under the

wind

beyond taut, jagged
curbside bushes,
rows upon rows
of yellowish green, summer fields
wavecrash
upon old rooftops
of grey and

black

all gone
into the hard, concrete asphalt
the cracked, bare distance
of an entire city

before the mute glass windows

Vindhyachal

Even now
this hill tucks the horizon
away
and carries the sun on its shoulder
the small red houses
on the terraced fields
the clouds snuggle on the sky-banks
a small white road climbs
to remind
the windmill to wave its hands
the wind carelessly crosses
the border between Urdu
and Hindi
and translates
seeds
to a spring

Untitled #72

Five crows, each

Qualifying each

Roots

the silver light pole

Before the drizzle

Sped trackways round the

Dark jeep engine

Black curb

to a friend in Shanghai quarantine

I don't know if hope
is something I have the right
to advise you
I don't know if I can still
point at the downwind seagulls and cavorting spindrifts
and tell you
look, look at them,
something profound
and nascent
is still happening
something like you
and me,
the fog encrusts the sanded beach whole
and all the pacific
muffles in a tenor of mayfly wing,
no, tomorrow
is history again,
you have to scream new screams
and cry the same cries,
with a dry throat,
about how the animals are dead
and the stars will not look
but all you wanted, those
who fumble and lie down
and scatter eclairs of hope around
all you wanted was for tomorrow
to be today, mundane, uncolored
and all we complain
is still the misty rain
sticky to our fence, the catkins
like a four year old, clingy to our hands
instead of the bright, April winds
that squeeze the whole spring through the teeth
of barbed wires, and left
live, reality-bleeding sighs
that never reach
the other side,

the other side of the ocean
is no longer hanging beside the sun
knitting the sea into sky,
the clouds broke
into a haze
and drove its thousand pale fingertips
gritting on these iron fences
and left undried tear marks
to be like
anyone's,
the other side of truth
is no longer lies, but whispers
murmured upon ear to ear
at sunforgotten corner of stairs
taking their humble, surprise rootlets
against eyes wide like daylight
that the other side of me,
is no longer you, but words, like
"I heard it's because people like you that.."
that people become less than people
and tears unrecognizable as tears
that the other side of hope
is no longer despair
but a helpless chuckle, the kind
only seen in museums, where
tragedy is better in distance
yet after which, they must get on
to another food scramble tomorrow
fictional, but always, real,
I am lucky to feel
the warmth of these tears down my cheeks
and this southernmost beach
of Shanghai, where I'm quarantined, with a city
shrouded in white
all behind,
when you said: "I don't have the luxury
to hope, but you—
you go, write your lines,
someone out there still

needs something as opaque
and as sparkling
as a poem."

At a New Shumai Shop in Hometown
After Miss Mo

when the chopsticks rested, the vase
is there, out of of the hot steam
a lady, leaning in the middle of it, arms
on a silk mat, like a pheasant, other
hand pluck the bonsai leaves, so
content her eyes, you'd think war
has ended for last time, below
chrysanthemums spatter, her
wavy dress, cyan the entire porcelain
and in between, almost invisible
a pair of bound, atrophied feet
the muffled, pain
of deep boudoir, glazed
for display on the dining table:
people throw toothpicks in it

Home, at last

this evening,   my
       sky is a forgetful   drunkard
           who beats
and beats my window
          all   red,
     with his   sunbled palms
     and seeing   those eyes
     behind blinds
     are not the ones   he's looking
        for (somehow   they've grown
old)   pleats the farside of night
into   lavender wafts of cirrus
 hiding   stars, like
   tears   between fingers:
I am sorry, stuck on my tongue
        are   the whole dark of night
and winters of homesickness
         nowhere to begin
nowhere to end.
          what is changed
      is not   a window of new   bamboo leaves
chisel lake surface   like a canvas
        into sunny reliefs   of wave rings,
      not   the two blades of a fresh clover
    holding off   the repaved asphalt
  from collapsing into one street,
        nor the remains of characters
      piling up   in the blackened basin
   grandma burned   for my safe return,
      nor stony steps beside river
    drench up a summer of heat
and night frog's singing
    upon which an old man tells me
"you don't remember me
but I saw you grew up here":
not them, no. but me
my looking upon them

knowing every look
will never be the same:
my present mythologized by the future,
and future ventriloquized by the past
        footprints on a beach
                chased by spindrifts
            smoothening out, each
              after each.

Saṃsāra

Every mid-summer noon on the lunar calendar,
we'd prepare a feast, laying out on the long table,
jade bowls and bamboo chopsticks on the wood plaque
a pair, a pair, a pair.
I, being playful, liked to climb
onto the empty chairs. And you, *Tia Tia*,
waved your banana-leaf fan,
your bamboo stool creaked. You smiled:
"come down, *Au-Siau*, the ancestors are yet to
return." I asked, if they are coming back,
why can't I see them? And you, *Tia Tia*,
stretching out a hand against the wind,
lighted up a red candle with another
flame, aflame,
Daylight's foot stretched long table.

Years passed. Daylight is shorter.
Again, the fake flowers to the side
wet your tombstone.
The fan on your stool
shivers in the wind.
I move it inside,
and place it among the chairs.
My palm is not big enough,
the candles flicker.
I lay out the bowls and chopsticks,
a pair, a pair, a pair,
a pair.

("Huí", to return, is not going back, but going through a different circle.)

One thousand ways of a foxtail in Pudong New Economic Zone

一

amid twelve forty-storied apartment buildings
the only thing that bows
in the wind

二

At noon, I feel the sun
burning up my nape
and a small beetle
refuging at my feet

三

O the unsightly dirt!
they call you "industrial waste"
and plant you
under a sightly cement:
you plant me

四

under the white sun
a foxtail
sweat green

五

a beetle on cement
leaftip
is as tall
as rooftop

in sunset
every dust mote
is clean
what does the garbageman
come to glean?

evening drizzles
on the broken tires
chirping,
a flock of birds

these misty carlights
ponderously the
rain

九

broken bikes falling each
on each
a last one nudge
my back

and the plain pale pang pounding pile driver

百

"What was the question?"
"A crack on the cement."

千

the wind
I listened
the sea
listens me

Acknowledgements

Several poems have been published previously in other magazines:

"Hwra" was published in *Reed Magazine*.

"The 3rd Graders Go to School" was published in *Ghost City Press*.

"PHOTONS" was published in *Meridian*.

"Samsara" was published in *Beyond World Literary Magazine*.

"Sunflower in Soup" was published in *Sunspot Lit*.

Colophon

Cover text is set in Onyx, Pristina, and Lora.
Interior texts are set in Lora and Ma Shan Zheng.

About Etchings Press

Etchings Press is a student-run publisher at the University of Indianapolis that runs a post-publication award—the Whirling Prize—as well as an annual publication contest for one poetry chapbook, one prose chapbook, and one novella. On occasion, Etchings Press publishes new chapbooks from previous winners. For more information about these contests and the Whirling Prize post-publication award, please visit etchings.uindy.edu.

Poetry
2023: *Other Side of Sea* by Xiaoqiu Qiu
2022: *A Place That Knows You* by Tiwaladeoluwa Adekunle
2022: *The Vaudeville Horse* by Elizabeth Kerlikowske
2021: *My Mother's Ghost Scrubs the Floor at 2 a.m.* by Robert Okaji
2020: *Vaginas Need Air* by Tori Grant Welhouse
2019: *As Lovers Always Do* by Marne Wilson
2018: *In the Herald of Improbable Misfortunes* by Robert Campbell
2017: *Uncle Harold's Maxwell House Haggadah* by Danny Caine
2016: *Some Animals* by Kelli Allen
2015: *Velocity of Slugs* by Joey Connelly
2014: *Action at a Distance* by Christopher Petruccelli

Prose
2023: *Leaving the House Unlocked* by Elizabeth Enochs (nonfiction)
2022: *Triple Point* by Laura Story Johnson (essays)
2021: *Bad Man Love Stories* by Curtis VanDonkelaar (fiction)
2020: *Three in the Morning and You Don't Smoke Anymore*
        by Peter J. Stavros (fiction)
2019: *Dissenting Opinion from the Committee for the Beatitudes*
        by Marc J. Sheehan (fiction)
2018: *The Forsaken* by Chad V. Broughman (fiction)
2017: *Unravelings* by Sarah Cheshire (memoir)
2016: *Pathetic* by Shannon McLeod (essays)
2015: *Ologies* by Chelsea Biondolillo (essays)
2014: *Static: Stories* by Frederick Pelzer (fiction)

Novella

2023: *Our Cadaver* by Elizabeth Toman
2022: *Goodbye to the Ocean* by Susan L. Lin
2021: *Miss Alma May Learns to Fight* by Stuart Rose
2020: *Under Black Leaves* by Doug Ramspeck
2019: *Savonne, Not Vonny* by Robin Lee Lovelace
2018: *Edge of the Known Bus Line* by James R. Gapinski
2017: *The Denialist's Almanac of American Plague and Pestilence*
      by Christopher Mohar
2016: *Followers* by Adam Fleming Petty

Chapbooks from Previous Winners

2022: *slighted...* by Chad V. Broughman (fiction)
2020: *Fruit Rot* by James R. Gapinski (fiction)
2016: #LOVESONG by Chelsea Biondolillo
      (microessays with photos and found text)

Xiaoqiu was born in Tongxiang, China. His native tongue is Wu Chinese and Mandarin. He started writing poetry in English when he was 25. After receiving a B.A. in English in Shanghai, he came to the United States for an M.A. in education at University of Michigan, Ann Arbor. He then switched to creative writing and earned an M.F.A. in poetry from UNLV. He is currently a Black Mountain Institute PhD fellow at UNLV. Visit xiaoqiu-qiu.com for more.